# Saving Grace

### A Journey of
### Hope and Healing

TAMMY K. BRADSHAW-SCOTT, PH.D.

WESTBOW
PRESS®
A DIVISION OF THOMAS NELSON
& ZONDERVAN

WestBow Press books may be ordered through booksellers or by contacting:

WestBow Press
A Division of Thomas Nelson & Zondervan
1663 Liberty Drive
Bloomington, IN 47403
www.westbowpress.com
1 (866) 928-1240

ISBN: 978-1-9736-7177-0 (sc)
ISBN: 978-1-9736-7176-3 (hc)
ISBN: 978-1-9736-7178-7 (e)

Library of Congress Control Number: 2019912493

Print information available on the last page.

WestBow Press rev. date: 9/13/2019

This book is dedicated to those who have lost a child or a loved one. May you find hope and healing in the Savior.

# Contents

# Introduction

## A Window into My Heart
## Our True Hope

I remember my affliction and my wandering, the bitterness and the gall. I well remember them, and my soul is downcast within me. Yet this I call to mind and therefore I have hope: Because of The Lord's great love we are not consumed, for His compassions never fail. They are new every morning; great is Your faithfulness. I say to myself, The Lord is my portion; therefore I will wait for Him. The Lord is good to those whose hope is in Him, to the one who seeks Him; it is good to wait quietly for the salvation of The Lord.

—Lamentations 3:19–26

Reflecting back on the bleak and stormy months of trying to save Rachel Grace, my youngest daughter, and the years following the unimaginable loss of her life, I am simply amazed that I have made it to the other side of such unbelievable devastation.

The heartbreak and the pain that I have lived through can never be fully articulated in a book, and there really are no words that can capture the full scope of the affliction of soul that I have experienced. The depths of suffering have forever changed the person I was, and I now relate to the world from a very different place. I have been surprised at how the loss of my child has changed me. It has done so in ways that I could not have imagined.

Throughout my life I have considered myself to be a strong and resilient individual—a person who does not give up easily. I have been that woman who keeps pushing forward no matter the headwinds that I face. And for those times when I tripped and stumbled, I always managed to get back up (by the grace of God). In truth, I have consistently thanked God over the years for the tenacity that He has graciously given me, enabling me to press forward in my journey.

Surrendering my life to Christ at age nineteen was just the beginning of my faith journey. Little did I know at that young age what God would do in my life as I placed my hope and my trust in Him. And little did I know that He would empower me to "soar on wings as eagles" through the many trials that I would face. Somehow I knew from the moment that I invited Him into my life that I would never be the same again.

My life has been amazingly and profoundly changed since that night so long ago when I invited Christ into my life to be my Lord and my Savior. And as I have walked through many trials and many storms, I have had no doubt that He would always keep His promise to me to "never leave me nor forsake me." And when I have felt absolutely alone in the wilderness of my own mind and soul, I have reached out to Him in utter desperation like the woman in the Bible who grabbed hold of the hem of Jesus's garment as He passed by her (she had suffered twelve years with a severe illness). He noticed her aloneness, her pain, and her suffering, and He honored her faith as she reached out to Him. He kept His promise.

After my decision to follow Jesus, I'd like to say that everything in my life was just wonderful, but if you've spent any amount of time in life, I think you know better. Just as you have, I have experienced numerous opportunities to become bitter and angry about the dark valleys, the fierce storms, and the deserts that I have had to walk through. And most definitely I have sensed the enemy of my soul lurking close by in those dark and lonely hours, whispering, "Poor you. After all your faithfulness to God, why would He allow this in your life?" I've heard many more taunts from the enemy baiting me to give up the fight, to give up my relationship with Christ. But from the beginning of surrendering my life to Christ, I chose to follow Him—and I continue to follow Him with each new day. In truth, God could take everything from me and I would still love, follow, and serve Him with my whole heart. I would probably scream, cry, pound my fists, and, like Peter, maybe even deny Him a time or two. But my heart echoes the words of Job: "Though He slay me yet will I praise Him."

From the very beginning of my surrender to Christ, my attitude has been "He is either my God or He is not—in the good times and in the bad times." When I have been at some of my lowest points, I have found myself going along while singing, "Jesus, Jesus, Jesus, there's just something about that name." And in those moments and days following the news of Rachel's death, my prominent thoughts and prayers were "Jesus, help!" My cry for help entered His ears. And though the nights have been long (and the days longer), and although the pain has been relentless, there is still another side to this story: hope!

After I gave my life to Christ, I began to read and study the

Bible (actually, I felt starved for the good news that the Bible offered), and I discovered the hope that we can have when we hold on to the promises found in God's Word. Over the years I have drawn much encouragement and renewal of my strength from God's Word. The Bible literally transformed my life from the inside out, teaching me the truth about my worth and the truth about His incredible love for me. The Bible is the most important and most valuable document or book that I could ever own because it speaks truth, instruction, and hope for my life.

For over thirty years, God has spoken to me through His Word. His Word has been "a lamp unto my feet and a light unto my path." And as I have walked through the horribleness of losing my daughter Rachel, God has spoken His love, truth, and mercies to my heart through His Word.

Each chapter of *Saving Grace* begins with a passage of scripture that God has impressed on my heart in a special way, and as I have walked through the various stages and years after losing Rachel, I have found comfort, strength, and hope in these passages. Throughout my journey, God has led me to many incredible scriptures in the Bible that have brought healing to my heart. One such passage is the one that I included at the beginning of this introduction from the book of Lamentations. I am especially comforted by the words in this verse: "His compassions never fail, they are new every morning; great is your faithfulness." This particular scripture has helped me to lift my head up off the pillow, put my feet on the floor, and move graciously into another day. These incredible words remind me that I am never alone in my suffering and my affliction, and that whatever I face in this life, the Lord my God goes with me.

This is what I believe with all my heart: we serve a mighty God, the Creator of this universe, who is always with us and has an unwavering, unconditional deep love for us. As the late Corrie ten Boom once said, "There is no pit so deep that God's love is not deeper still." The truth is, when we have surrendered our hearts and lives to Christ, of whom the Father says, "There is no other way to the Father but through Him," the impossible can happen. God has enabled me to get up and do the impossible countless times over the course of my faith journey, and He has shown me that His love is much deeper than the dark pit of losing my child.

My friend, as you journey forward on your road to healing, I pray that you too will discover that "He is good to those whose hope is in Him." And may you experience His amazing grace as He lifts you up out of your pit of pain and suffering. My sincere prayer is that you will discover the hope that is found in God's love and that, as you continue to trust in Him, no matter what, the Lord will redeem all the loss and devastation that you have lived through.

Blessings to you and yours.

# Chapter 1

## And the Storm Began

But when he saw how strong the wind was he became frightened; and, beginning to sink, he cried out, Lord save me. Immediately Jesus stretched out His hand and caught him, O you of little faith, why did you doubt?

—Matthew 14:30–31

The words I heard from the other end of the telephone line are forever embedded in the walls of my memory: *"Jay has been beating Rachel!"*

My body began trembling as I stood frozen in the middle of my front room. Rachel, my youngest, in an abusive relationship? How could this be? Thoughts filled with horrible images overwhelmed my mind. This call would mark the start of a storm I could never have imagined.

## "Lord, Save Me"

Weak and sick to my stomach, I desperately begged the caller for details and for assurance that my daughter was safe. The woman (a friend of Rachel's) on the other end of the line assured me that Rachel was safe in a women's shelter. As I imagined my daughter living in a situation that had forced her into a shelter for battered women, I felt the darkness like a crushing wave pounding down on top of me. The room spun around me as panic filled my heart. *How could this be happening, and how could anyone hurt Rachel? She's so kind, thoughtful, and compassionate toward others, frequently putting others' needs above her own.*

Standing alone in my apartment hundreds of miles away from my daughter, I determined I would leave immediately to bring her safely home. Then, a condemning voice shouted in my head, *Why are you so far away from your girl in the first place? Why are you here while she is there?*

Standing in my beautifully furnished apartment located in one of the most coveted spots in all of San Diego, I felt more alone than ever. The apartment, and the classy furnishings inside, belonged to my friends who had offered to rent it to me while I completed a one-year internship in the area as part of my clinical psychology doctoral program. The apartment was conveniently located between my school and my internship site. It was perfect.

The apartment was truly lovely, and from my balcony on the seventh floor I could see all the sailboats in the marina below. The smell of Italian food from Little Italy's restaurants that lined the touristy streets poured in through my windows at the start of each new day.

Even amid all this beauty and surrounding activity, I found that living in a large city with one-way streets (and virtually no street parking) took some getting used to. The best way that I could imagine to become familiar with my surroundings was to run through the different areas of the city (driving the area was a little overwhelming at first). I have enjoyed running most of my life, and I have certainly enjoyed particular areas to run in, San Diego now being rated as my new favorite location.

Many of my friends and my grown daughters loved to visit me. We enjoyed the restaurants, shops, and tourist attractions. But misery lingered! One evening I telephoned one of my daughters. She was living in Los Angeles at the time. Crying, I expressed how much I missed her and her sisters and explained that this was the first time I had lived so far away from them. With an encouraging tone, my daughter shared with me that this was a time I should enjoy. All my kids were grown, and my time was now my own. But I loved the mom role more than anything in the world. Truthfully, I had not planned on attending school or obtaining a career. I loved the job I had as a mom and a wife. But life happens and plans change.

Divorced and now a single mom of three daughters—not exactly what I had planned on for my future—I found myself in this spot after thirteen years of marriage, being a stay-at-home mom and a homeschooler of my three daughters. So, with no prior college education or job skills to enable employment, I enrolled as a full-time college student at a local community college. As the years rolled past, I worked at and struggled with keeping the balance as a full-time single mom and a full-time student.

It is amazing how one day you look up, mistakes and all, and your children are grown and they no longer need you. San Diego was my "looking up" moment: I was alone in a gorgeous city, living in my friends' apartment, with daughters no longer needing me (in the way that our children need us when they are young and under our care). So I did what all parents do with an empty nest—I cried a lot! And when I wasn't crying, I worked very hard at accepting my unexpected place in life, now as a woman with a college education and an evolving career.

Part of accepting my life as a single woman with grown children was the need to have a plan of action, such as where I would live after my internship and what job I would look for, among a multitude of other life details. But as many of us know, we can make our plans with the best of intentions, but then that phone call comes, and everything changes in an instant.

That phone call came for me in my San Diego apartment. The caller informed me of my daughter's situation, and she assured me that Rachel was okay. The woman also reassured me that Rachel would call me from the shelter—then she hung up the phone. I stood, cell phone in hand, waiting. Within minutes, Rachel called.

Something in my nineteen-year-old daughter's voice alarmed me. Over the phone and from the battered-women's shelter, Rachel, with a pleading voice, explained, "It's not his fault. He is sick. He never meant to hurt me." The only response that I thought might be helpful in that moment was to assure her that I understood and that I would be there to help her. But inside, my heart broke as I listened to my daughter rationalize her fiancé's behavior.

Now with increased desperation, I persistently asked Rachel for the location of the shelter, and I asked if I may bring her home. But she incessantly repeated, "It's not his fault." I felt helpless. With hundreds of miles separating us, I just wanted to reach through the phone and bring Rachel home. Thankfully, after several minutes of conversation, she told me the location of the shelter and asked me to come get her. Thank You, Jesus!

Immediately I made the proper arrangements to take a leave from my internship. And after filling my gas tank and picking up Rachel's father, I made the five-hour drive to bring my daughter safely home. In my angst to get to Rachel, I broke a few speed laws along the way. I remember a very kind highway patrol officer pulling me over. Once I explained the situation my daughter was in, he gave me a warning to slow down in order to arrive safely for my daughter. He shared with me that his daughter had once been in the same situation as my daughter, so he understood the fear that a parent experiences in such a circumstance.

My heart was filled with fear almost the entire drive as I imagined Rachel in the most horrible situation. The closer I got to the shelter, the more I mentally prepared myself, and the more I prayed for the strength to handle whatever condition I would find Rachel in.

Immense relief filled my heart the moment I saw Rachel approaching the car, carrying a large box of her personal belongings. Feeling consoled with my daughter safe in my car, I experienced yet more relief as I observed no physical injuries on Rachel's face. However, this *is* what this mother's eyes did see in her daughter's face—a broken and confused young woman living a life of violence and trauma that had brought the innocence of her childhood to an abrupt end.

## We Can Do the Impossible

Now that I had my daughter securely in my car and heading in the direction of home, I saw the storm clouds. The raging storm came into full view right in front of me. Looking over my shoulder from the driver's seat, I sat stunned by how Rachel's face told the story. With confusion and anguish deeply etched into her pale, thin face, I witnessed an intense and passionate struggle as we drove away from the place where she had dreamed of building a life with her fiancé. We literally drove away from her dreams.

From the time that Rachel was a young girl, she had had a

desire to have children and become a mom. She thought of pregnant women as very beautiful, and she had pictures of expectant mothers on her bedroom walls. Rachel had, in fact, realized her dream for a moment. She became pregnant while living out of state with her fiancé, but tragically, she lost the baby just a few weeks prior to her stay at the shelter. Rachel was absolutely devastated and heartbroken at the loss of her unborn child. Now that dream moved farther away as the distance in miles grew between us and her fiancé.

Rachel's countenance grew with panic; the farther we drove, the more distressed she became. Clearly, leaving her fiancé proved much more frightening and overwhelming for her than I had anticipated. What emotional destruction had Rachel been living with? She would need a lot of care and professional help to heal from the domestic violence she had lived with for five months. But first things first: she would need a medical checkup immediately.

Unsure of what physical injuries she had sustained, I set an appointment for a thorough medical evaluation. But unfortunately and sadly, we never made it to the medical appointment. Within a couple of days of my bringing Rachel back home, she left with her fiancé back out of state, out of the reach of her family and friends.

*Dial again. Nope, no answer. Maybe try another text. ... No response! Why won't she respond?* My head screamed so loudly that I didn't know if I had spoken the words or just thought the words. What is happening to her? I cannot stand this. God, please help me. I fear I am losing my mind.

When I could not contact Rachel, the relentless nightmares began, filling me with fear and panic upon waking. During the day I couldn't focus on anything. I began filling my thoughts with ways to kidnap her and take her away to someplace safe. I researched laws pertaining to domestic violence and the rights of family members, and I quickly discovered that families have no rights when it comes to domestic violence.

After several days of receiving no response and no word from Rachel, I called the police near where she and her fiancé lived and requested a welfare check. Yes, she was there, and apparently her condition was satisfactory to the police. But had they really checked and made sure she was okay, or had they just poked their heads into the apartment and made a quick, and inaccurate, assessment that "she's fine"? *Now what do I do?* Feeling completely powerless and unable to help, I recognized my desperate need to go before the Lord and cry out to Him. (I am not sure why we go to the Lord as a last resort.)

God spoke very clearly and specifically to my heart that night, reminding me of the passage in Matthew where Jesus called Peter out of the boat to walk on the water to Him. Peter obeyed, and he began walking to Jesus (what an amazing experience that must have been for Peter, doing the impossible for his Lord). I cannot imagine what a beautiful and amazing sight it must have been: a simple human man following the direction of his God and doing something that he'd never imagined possible. Initially after stepping out of the boat, Peter managed to stay above water, but when he took his eyes off Jesus, looking at the raging storm instead, he sank down into the storm. The Lord showed me that night, through His mercy and grace, that I am a Peter, sinking in my storm. Instead of looking at my Lord, I had given the storm my full attention, and it threatened to pull me under.

That night God turned me around and lifted me up out of the storm. God knew the direction the storm was heading, and He knew that this would be the most powerful and destructive storm that I would ever face. That night God impressed on my heart that He would enable me to do the impossible if I kept my eyes fixed on Him. And that night I learned the meaning of "the calm before the storm."

# Chapter 2

## Why This, God?

Find rest, O my soul, in God alone; my hope comes
from Him. He alone is my rock and my salvation;
He is my fortress, I will not be shaken.

—Psalm 62:5–6

At last, the long-awaited call came. Finally Rachel had left Jay, her abusive fiancé. Her friend also informed me that Rachel was driving cross-country toward home, assuring me that she would keep me posted on Rachel's whereabouts. In that moment, indescribable relief filled my heart, and I desperately longed to see my daughter.

Repeatedly and anxiously I checked my phone, hoping to receive word of Rachel's location and her condition. Rachel's friend called and told me that she had arrived safely in town and was staying with a different friend. With great restraint, I determined that I would not call or text Rachel. I did not want to betray the friend who had kept this mama mercifully and graciously informed. So I waited all day and all night, but no message came from Rachel. As the night moved on, my thoughts became very dark once again as I faced the reality that she may again return to the abusive situation. *Please, no, Lord Jesus.*

Rachel's call never came. The call that did come, however, took my breath from me and forced me to pull my car over to the side of the freeway. Rachel's fiancé's mom had called me. Her voice sounded calm but lifeless and troublingly devoid of emotion (this poor mother was clearly in a state of shock). She told me in a matter-of-fact tone that Rachel had left Jay the previous day and that he had hung himself early that morning.

Sitting in my car on the side of the freeway, flooded with perplexing emotions, I sobbed uncontrollably. The only words that I could utter to Jay's mom were "I am so very sorry." Conflicting emotions continued to compete for my attention.

In my heart I felt relief that Jay would no longer be able to harm Rachel, but that relief gave way to crushing feelings of guilt and shame. Why would I experience relief following the news of this young man's death? I couldn't stop crying. My heart broke for Jay, who had struggled with, and agonized over, the harsh reality of living with a complex and difficult mental illness. Now he had taken his own life. I was heartsick.

In the weeks and months that followed Jay's death, I watched my young daughter grapple with a situation that most older, more mature adults would find, at the very least, debilitating. The road ahead would be one of great pain. This path would be a dark, lonely, and wearisome journey.

Following Jay's memorial service, Rachel left with his parents out of state to visit the site where he would be buried. Following the visit to the cemetery, Rachel attempted suicide in a hotel room where she and Jay had once stayed together.

The sheriff's call came well after midnight. Awakening from a deep sleep at the buzz of my cell phone, I listened to the officer and tried to make sense of what he was saying. The officer kept repeating, "Ma'am, your daughter is hurting. She needs help." Shaking off grogginess, I felt panic rising in my chest, and I insisted on the details: "What does that mean? Where is she? What has happened to her?" The officer responded to my alarm with an empathetic voice: "Ma'am, your daughter is in the hospital, but she needs help." I made the necessary arrangements and planned to make the trip out of state once again.

As I drove in the early morning light to visit my daughter in a psychiatric hospital, I prayed once again for God to prepare my heart and provide me with the strength to face whatever I would need to face. The four-hour drive I experienced was both solemn and prayerful. In my weariness, I recognized my desperate need of God's wisdom for the path that lay ahead. My heart pounded as I walked through the double doors of the hospital's entrance.

Within minutes of my signing into the psychiatric unit as a visitor, a very thin-framed Rachel came walking into the visitors' room to greet me. Clothed in a green hospital gown with bandages wrapped around both arms, she hugged me. Her hazel eyes looked green with the backdrop of pale skin framed by shoulder-length red hair. Even her loose curls appeared unkempt and weary. My heart suffered immense sorrow as I saw the condition of my daughter. What had happened to her?

> I felt your heartbreak. I felt your pain.
> I saw you there. I saw the whole thing!

Upon Rachel's release from the hospital, she came to stay with me for a few days in my San Diego apartment. I'll never forget one night in particular when she turned in for the night on the couch. Leaning over to tuck her in with a blanket, I was struck by the look in her eyes. Her eyes were a window into her heart, and in them I saw deep pain, sorrow, and loss. I also saw brokenness, the type of brokenness that occurs when the human mind has experienced overwhelming circumstances and those circumstances have become too much to handle. I have worked with patients over the years in psychiatric hospitals with that same brokenness in their eyes—heartbreaking! When I saw the extreme and serious condition of Rachel that night, I realized that she would need help to heal and recover from the trauma that she had experienced, and I knew right then that I needed to be available for my daughter in the many capacities that she would need me.

Packed and ready, I left my apartment and my psychology internship behind in San Diego. Within a couple of weeks, Rachel and I moved to a city where she had fond memories and connections from her childhood. I had little money at this time, so I borrowed enough money from my brother for a deposit and our first month's rent. When Rachel and I first moved into our small rental home, we had no furniture with the exception of our beds. We used an ice chest as our refrigerator and ate our meals sitting on the kitchen counter (which we actually enjoyed). I purchased two beanbag chairs for our front room. But the slimness of our material condition did not matter. All that mattered to me was my daughter's safety. When Rachel had asked if I would move and if she could live with me, I knew that this was a blessing and a gift from God. I did not know how I would provide for our needs, but I knew that my daughter needed her mama.

God's timing has always amazed me! After we settled in our home, God opened a door for me to secure a full-time job at a local behavioral health hospital as a clinical therapist. This position would be exactly what I needed to financially provide for us, and with the hospital's location so near to our home, I could drive home and spend my lunch hour with Rachel.

During this healing and restorative period, I definitely felt weariness in my spirit, mind, and body. I tried so hard to help and desperately wanted to lift the burden off Rachel's shoulders, but I often felt powerless to help my own daughter. All that I could do was pray for her, listen to her as she shared her immense pain, and hold her in the middle of the night. Some nights she would climb into bed with me, and I would wrap my mommy arms around her as she cried herself to sleep. In the evening hours after work, Rachel and I would sit on our front patio, and there she would pour out her pain, anger, and self-blame. But little I said or did brought comfort to Rachel in those hours, days, and months following Jay's death. I'm not sure that there is anything more agonizing than watching your child suffer and feeling like you are unable to help her.

Another suicide attempt followed with another psychiatric hospitalization. Rachel demonstrated symptoms of posttraumatic stress disorder (PTSD) and major depression, and she desperately needed psychiatric treatment. As a therapist at that time, I had had significant experience working with patients diagnosed with a wide range of mental health disorders, including PTSD and depression. Based on my training, I was aware of the type of treatment Rachel needed. Unfortunately, she was not open to taking medications during that period, but thankfully Rachel agreed to see a therapist once per week. Eventually she went twice per week and began to improve.

Rachel experienced some blessed high points, but relentless dark periods always followed. During the darkest times I frequently had nightmares of Rachel in horrible situations. One night I dreamed of an attacker hurting her, and in the dream I could literally hear the sound of her being hit. Not yet awake, I grabbed a wooden post from my bed frame and started toward her room. Thankfully, I awoke before she could see her crazy mother ready to beat the tar out of the stranger in my dream.

As Rachel continued in therapy, she developed a wonderful trusting relationship with her therapist, and she appeared to be making good progress. Rachel also began to talk positively about her future and her desire to attend medical school to become an obstetrician. What amazing joy and relief I felt. And I actually began sleeping through the night again.

One afternoon, Rachel and I took a "field trip" to the university where I was teaching as an adjunct professor. I will always remember sitting behind her in the touring cart as one of the students drove us around the campus. Rachel looked so happy, so hopeful, so much like my girl.

Following our tour and visit, Rachel began to work on an entrance letter in preparation to attend the university. As I read her entrance letter per her request, I smiled at her giftedness as a writer. Encouraged and hopeful, I continued taking Rachel to her twice-weekly therapy appointments.

After a therapy session one afternoon, Rachel came out quite perky to meet me in the parking lot. She stated, "I think I'm ready to move on, Mom." I almost screamed with excitement right there in my car, but I contained myself and simply hugged and squeezed her.

As with any and all journeys, there are starts and stops along the way. Rachel's journey was filled with unpredictability. She would dip down so low and then rebound back up—the proverbial emotional roller coaster. But day by day, she appeared to be improving, and that is all I dared hope for. Rachel began to hang out with friends again, and she made some wonderful new friends, getting her out of the house and allowing for further healing. Rachel also started participating in other positive activities, like attending a college-aged church group one night a week and going to movies with friends. I also noticed that her Bible reappeared on the nightstand next to her bed.

One of Rachel's new friends captured a lot of her time and attention, and she spent increasing amounts of time on social media with her new acquaintance. Rachel had no romantic interest in him but stated that they shared a lot in common. One evening she invited him over to meet me. The moment I saw the young man, serious concerns filled my heart. With his flat affect and the hopelessness in his eyes, I immediately knew why Rachel had connected with this new friend. My previous encouragement evaporated, and I once again feared for my daughter.

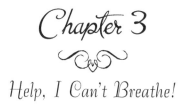

# Chapter 3

## Help, I Can't Breathe!

My grace is sufficient for you, for my power is made perfect in weakness.

—2 Corinthians 12:9

Rachel spent increasing amounts of time with her new acquaintance, and she moved farther away from recovery and spiraled back down into despair. I encouraged her to spend time with other friends, friends who were positive and encouraging, but not many people understood what she was going through. How could they? Oftentimes when we do not understand the struggles or circumstances someone is going through, we tend to avoid them or pull away. And we also pull away from people ourselves when we have gone through extraordinary difficulties because we know that people will not understand our pain and struggle. This is what happened with Rachel. She pulled away from people following Jay's death, which led to deep loneliness. No longer an average teenage girl whose greatest concerns centered on friendships and which college to attend, she no longer fit in with those who were at her stage of life.

Rachel had experienced overwhelming trauma that,

consequently, dramatically changed her perspective of others and of life in general. And she could not relate with the trivialities kids her age complained of. Friends became scarce because they did not understand her pain and loss. So when Rachel met someone who could relate with her pain, she no longer felt so alone. But what I did not realize was that her friendship with this young man would have a destructive and devastating end.

## "My Grace Is Sufficient for You"

On the last night I saw Rachel, she told me that she was going to hang out with her new friend. I questioned her and asked her to please reconsider since she was still recovering from the flu. She insisted that she was fine. In fact, she seemed surprisingly energetic and happy. She wished me a good night through a crack in her bedroom door. I told her that I loved her, and I went to bed.

Waking up early the next morning and following my usual pattern, I went to check on Rachel. Her bed lay unmade, her laptop was open from use the night before, and her dog, Shadow, lay happily sleeping in her usual place on the bed. But I saw no trace of Rachel. Initially I experienced no alarm because, in times past, she had stayed overnight at friends' homes when the hour was late and she was too tired to drive home. So I resumed my morning routine.

With my running shoes on, I headed out the door. Forty-five minutes into my run and nearly home, I stopped suddenly as I heard the following words in my heart: *You have two daughters now, not three.* What clear and unmistakable words. I cannot explain this moment, but to this day I still remember hearing them. I leaned forward with my hands resting on my knees, standing there on a freeway overpass, trying to make sense of what I had just heard. Taking a deep breath, I resumed my run home.

As I approached my driveway, I noticed a note on our front door. Taking the note from the door, I read the words, "Dear Miss Bradshaw, please contact the San Bernardino Sheriff's Department regarding your daughter Rachel." Having no idea what this could be about, I walked around the side of our house, located a hidden key, and began to let myself in. As I inserted the key into the keyhole, I heard a woman's voice behind me.

"Miss Bradshaw," her voice called out. I turned around to face the person addressing me. The officer, who was accompanied by my neighbor, approached me in my driveway. She stated that she needed to speak with me about my daughter Rachel. I immediately asked, "Is she okay?" The officer stated flatly, "No, ma'am, she is not." Stunned, and without hesitation, I replied with the question "Is she alive?" Then came the words that no parent can ever imagine hearing: "No, ma'am, she is not!" Reactively, I collapsed on the concrete step beneath me. Feeling my own life slipping from me, I wailed and sobbed.

As I sat on the cold concrete step, my caring neighbor placed cold towels on my neck and forehead. The officer asked several questions in rapid succession, or so it seemed that way at that moment. My neighbor had to remind her to give me a minute to breathe because I had just been given the news of my daughter's death. The officer softened, gave me a moment, then asked if there was anyone I wanted her to call. Rachel's dad was called first, then my other two daughters. Sitting there in shock over Rachel's death, I experienced myself standing outside of the most terrible and unimaginable scene—like a horrified spectator watching from the sidelines.

Homicide detectives arrived on the scene shortly after I received the news of Rachel's death (I cannot be certain of the exact time frame because of the level of shock I experienced). Police detectives were an overwhelming presence in our small home. Initially, I did not understand why they were there, and I was surprised to see them in Rachel's bedroom going through her belongings. Another female homicide detective asked most of the questions. She was thoughtful and kind. She shared with me that she also had a daughter and could not imagine what I was going through. At some point during this time, she handed me the ring that Rachel had been wearing. It was her engagement ring to Jay.

The lead homicide detective informed me that at 4:35 a.m., Rachel was killed as a passenger in a car accident. She continued to explain that the car had hit a concrete-embedded traffic light pole at approximately seventy miles per hour. Rachel, my youngest daughter, had been pronounced dead at the scene.

The driver (her friend whom she had left with the night before), on the other hand, had survived. The on-scene emergency crews extracted him from the demolished car and transported him to a local hospital. He would make a full recovery. The detective also informed me that they were investigating the nature of the car accident. The evidence at the accident scene led investigators to suspect that this "accident" was an intentional act on the part of the driver.

In addition to the shock of being told that my daughter had been killed, I now found myself in the agonizing position of trying to sort out confusing and disturbing details. My mind now grappled with what had really happened in those early morning hours. Was my daughter's death a murder?

In the early hours and days following Rachel's death, a heavy fog of denial and disbelief encircled me. How I wish that I had

had more clarity in those moments. But when you are in a state of shock, you simply do not possess the capacity to think clearly. Though my mind fought for understanding, and with my heart completely broken, in the quietness of my spirit I could hear God's voice: "My grace is sufficient for you." In the days, weeks, and years to follow, I would experience my God's grace in ways that would carry me through the darkest nights of my soul.

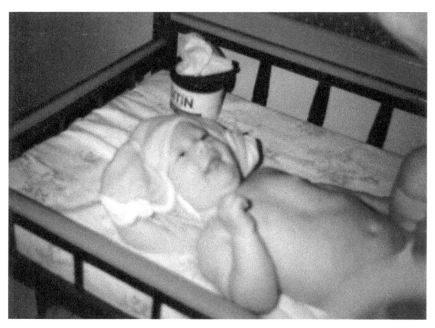

*Baby Rachel and Mommy being silly during a diaper change.*

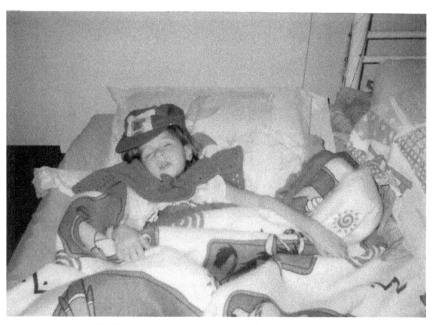

*Rachel, about four years old, fell asleep with her hat and cape on, and with her favorite* Lion King *blanket.*

*Rachel, age five. She always took care of her stuffed fur babies.*

*Rachel at age six. Her favorite playtime activity*
*often involved playing the little mama.*

*On the local swim team. Rachel was a natural in the water.*

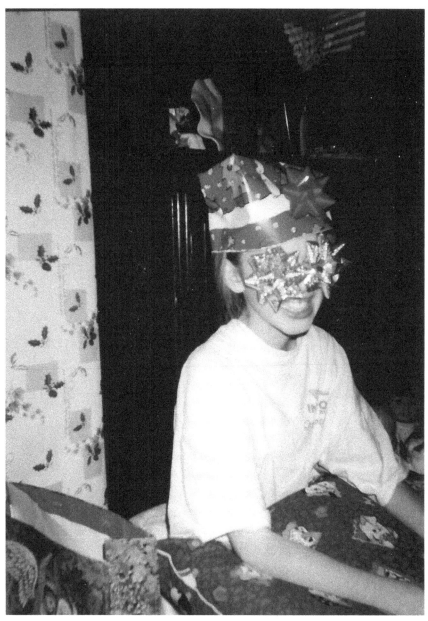

*Birthday time for this little nine-year-old. Rachel had a very funny sense of humor, as she is demonstrating here.*

*Rachel loved playing dress-up and acting silly.*

*Rachel enjoyed dance and performing. This dance outfit is one she wore for a show she was in.*

*Rachel was part of the AWANA Club. She's displaying*
*awards that she earned for memorizing scripture.*

*Rachel is about age twelve here. She was always a lover of animals. Here she is with one of her newborn kittens.*

*One of my favorite times with Rachel at Knott's Berry Farm.*

*Rachel was a beautiful young woman. She eventually grew taller than me, her mom.*

*The coolness of being a Teenager, but she still enjoyed
setting up the nativity scene at Christmas*

*Rachel's first prom in 9<sup>th</sup> grade, I love this moment with her.*

*Birthday dinner, 18, with one of her best friends, and still silly!*

*Age 19 and beautiful*

*Putting on stage make-up before a theater performance*

*Rachel performed in many live performances at LifeHouse Theater. She was beautiful to watch on stage – I never tired of watching her perform.*

*This is how I remember Rachel's face, her smile could light up a room.
This photo was taken shortly before she was living with the trauma
of domestic violence and before she experienced her losses.*

# Chapter 4

## But I Don't Want to Get Up

When Jesus saw him lying there and learned that
he had been in this condition for a long time, He
asked him, do you want to get well?

—John 5:6

$\mathcal{F}$ollowing the funeral and memorial services for Rachel, family and friends left and resumed their lives. I, on the other hand, curled up in a ball in my bed. I did not want to get up, and it hurt to breathe. I no longer wanted to "do life." My once-held desires for life quickly evaporated into a colorless existence.

When family and friends came to offer their condolences, I struggled to receive comfort. Have you ever hurt so badly that you refused comfort? Up to this point in my life, I had never felt pain so deeply that I refused comfort from others. But having experienced such a tragic loss as the death of my child, I could now identify with the scene in the New Testament after King Herod slaughtered all the baby boys age two and under. Though Herod's foolish attempts to kill Jesus failed, the outcry of pain could be heard throughout the city. "A voice heard in Ramah, weeping and great mourning, Rachel weeping for her children and refusing to be comforted, because they are no more" (Matthew 2:18). Now when I read this passage of scripture, I feel deeply and personally for these mothers—because my child is no more.

After Rachel's passing, I found that sitting in her bedroom provided some comfort, but it also proved to be equally painful. I would lie on her bed, take in her scent, and wish she would walk through the door. In those early days, I could hear her voice in my sleep and in my waking hours, saying, "Mom." Most nights my sleep included nightmares about Rachel dying and me attempting different ways to prevent her death. I always failed. Then there were the nightmares of terrible incidents happening to my other two daughters. Again, in my dreams I failed to save them. The dreams and nightmares were tormenting, to say the very least. But after receiving prayer from a lovely friend, by the grace of God my nightmares stopped.

Though many folks were praying for me and my family, I struggled terribly with my desire to "do life." I did not want to finish my doctorate program, I did not want to return to work as a therapist, and I did not want to spend time interacting with people. I seriously wondered if I would ever be interested in engaging in life again, and I really did not know if I would ever be okay.

After losing a child or loved one, is it possible that we never regain our "self" and our life as we knew it before our loss? Was it possible that I would remain a hollow shell of a woman, never coming back to life? These thoughts overwhelmed my mind every day after Rachel passed away. But in truth, I didn't care anymore. I was sinking, and I had no desire to come back up, or so I thought. Entirely unsure of what normal emotions I should be experiencing, I struggled to navigate my emotions from day to day. I also experienced a period of disconnection between myself,

God, and people. Not that God and people went anywhere, but that emotionally I moved away. I just wanted to lie down next to Rachel and never get up. But I also had the presence of mind to know that my other two daughters needed me to live—and they needed me to be well.

## "Do You Want to Get Well?"

Frankly, I was very upset that I "had to be okay," and I could not at that time imagine how I would ever feel any differently. But Jesus had spoken to my heart that His grace would be sufficient for me—but was it? Was this His grace I was experiencing? If it was, it sure didn't feel like His grace. Throughout my years of serving Christ, I have been very aware that He allows us to make our own choices, even when they are not what is best for us. And throughout my adult life as a Christian, I have had many opportunities to do my own thing and go my own way. It would be great if I could say that I have always walked perfectly and have always responded to God's direction for my life, but I haven't. So as I saw what was before me—the pain, the suffering, the journey—I had a directional choice to make. And I was keenly aware that God would not force me to get up and move forward if I chose not to. But as I pondered the times when I had not chosen God's best for me, His path, I was reminded of the misery I experienced each and every time.

What did God's direction in this situation look like for me? And what long-term effects would the loss of Rachel have on me and my life? At the time, all I could see was blackness and deep pain with no way of escape. But God showed me a way of escape, and that way is found in the words of Jesus to the paralytic man in the book of John. I have always been puzzled and struck by the question Jesus poses to the man in this passage: "Do you want to get well?" I'm thinking, *Well, yes. Who wouldn't want to go from being paralyzed to walking—right?* John points out in this passage that Jesus knew the man had been in this condition for a long time—over thirty years. This man had grown accustomed to living with this health condition. In fact, his paralysis was a large part of his identity. How could it not be? He had been relating to the world for over thirty years as a paralytic man, and the town knew him as such. He also made his living as a paralytic man because he could not work performing physical labor. What else could he do?

Can you imagine what the implications would be for this man suddenly to regain his ability to walk? We assume that this would be amazing, and in its own right it would be, but consider how his healing would change his life. He would now have to work for his living, instead of relying on others to show mercy and give to him. And given this man had been disabled for such a long time, we can be pretty certain that he was lacking in skills and work experience. Even more profoundly, this poor fellow's entire perspective on himself, his life, and the world around him would now need to change. No wonder Jesus asked him if he wanted to get well. Getting up from his paralyzed position would require faith and a lot of courage.

In my work as a therapist, I have experienced this same situation with my patients and clients—but instead of a physical paralysis, they have psychological paralysis. Many of these folks have walked around for years with massive psychological wounds that have crippled them, and they cannot imagine life without these wounds. Their psychological disabilities have become their identity, and they have adjusted their lifestyles accordingly. To imagine living free from the paralysis is simply too overwhelming for many people. And honestly, without Christ, I can understand why.

Now the turn is mine. I hear Jesus asking the question in my heart. What will my answer be? Will I continue to lie in my bed and allow myself to be swallowed up in the pain? Will I allow myself to be a woman whose sole identity is built on the loss of her child? Jesus will never force me, or you, to get up. And He will never force healing upon us. The choice is always up to us. But to be sure, whenever He calls us or invites us to a place, including a place of healing, the journey is always incredible. As I have already shared, I have lived with the misery of not following God's best for me, and that is no fun. So, I said yes to Jesus and yes to His healing power in my life. And by His grace, I got up!

# Chapter 5

## Under the Gavel of Guilt and Shame

I waited patiently for the Lord, He turned to me
and heard my cry. He lifted me out of the slimy pit,
out of the mud and mire; He set my feet on a rock
and gave me a firm place to stand. He put a new
song in my mouth, a hymn of praise to our God.

—Psalm 40:1–3

Getting up was just the beginning. The road to healing would also mean that I would need strength and courage to face the daunting, unrelenting faces of guilt and shame.

If you are a parent, then you, like all parents, have experienced a case of "would've, could've, should've" when your children enter into adulthood. Most parents have the opportunity to make right the silly and stupid mistakes that they have made throughout the years of raising their children. However, if your child dies before you have the opportunity to right those wrongs with your child, you are left with unfinished business. And unfortunately, unfinished business can prevent closure from happening, which in turn interferes with the process of healing and forgiveness.

Have you ever spoken with a parent who said that they did

a perfect job of raising their kids? No, I haven't either. Certainly some parents make better choices when raising their children than other parents do, but I have found that this is most often the result of better experiences and circumstances when they themselves were growing up, that is, a two-parent home, economic stability, the absence of physical, sexual, and/or emotional abuse, and the absence of drug and/or alcohol abuse (I'll save this topic for another book).

Every parent has made his or her fair share of parental mistakes. No parent is perfect, and living mistake-free is simply not possible. And remember, the only perfect person is God the Father, Jesus the Son of God, and the Holy Spirit.

The problem is that when we carry around the lie of having to be perfect, we are at great risk of being assaulted by guilt and shame. And when we believe the lie that we have failed to be what every parent, sibling, family member, or friend "should" do or be, we can sink into a very dark pit of guilt and shame. The pit of guilt and shame, in my opinion, is one of the most destructive pits that we can sink into.

Soon after hearing the news of Rachel's passing, I felt the weight of guilt coming down on me like a judge's gavel pounding down on the guilty criminal in a courtroom. Then angry voices shouted in my head: *It's your fault, it's your fault, it's your fault!* My own voice shouted these accusations. My thoughts falsely accused me, *You could have done so much more to help her. Why didn't you? Because you are a failure as a parent. That's why she died.* These thoughts were relentless. And I was not in a place to dispute them—because I believed them.

Many wonderful people at my place of employment reached out to me, surrounding me with support and loving-kindness. After I returned to work about six weeks later, the physicians and residents were especially attentive to what I was going through and what I most needed. One female physician resident in particular was extremely kind and reached out to me. She invited me to an exercise class with the goal in mind of getting me connected again with others. So after many excuses for why I could not go, I finally said yes.

I'll never forget the experience of utter disappointment in myself and anger toward myself. As the exercise music began and the class members were excited and ready to go, I felt the excitement that I had experienced over the years of attending and teaching aerobics classes. Within seconds, this excitement was replaced with overwhelming sense of guilt and shame. *How dare I enjoy this class, or anything, while my daughter lies in her grave?!* Needless to say, I did not go back. I was very angry at myself. I despised myself to the point of not wanting to eat or breathe air into my lungs.

Here is the point where I must be very honest with my readers. To do otherwise would be to defeat the purpose of *Saving Grace*. And the purpose of *Saving Grace* is to help you walk through your dark valley and come through to the other side with hope and healing. In honesty and transparency, I confess to you that I despaired of life, and I experienced depression, anxiety, and fleeting thoughts of suicide. I knew that I could not allow myself to entertain thoughts of suicide; this would have been very dangerous. I also knew that the enemy of my soul, Satan, wanted me to self-destruct. So I determined to immerse myself in God's Word. I needed to fill my mind with what God had said was true about me, and I knew from His Word that I would receive strength and courage.

Most people did not know about the dark thoughts in my head. I did not share my thoughts or struggles, for the most part, because I feared being judged. Where was my faith? Didn't I know that God has forgiven me for all the mistakes that I have made as a mom? But unfortunately, my mind was constantly flooded with all the things that I should have done differently. In fact, my mind would not allow me to think about any of the good or positive things that I'd done as a mom. During this treacherous time, the good and wonderful acts that I performed as a mom did not exist. Instead, every memory that came to mind and every destination that I visited led back to negative and regretful thoughts. This dark pit of guilt and shame went on for months and even years. I could not climb out of the darkness. As I stumbled around in this dark place, the enemy chimed in, hurling accusations and reminding me of all my sins. And I passively agreed. Oh, how low I sank!

While I was in this very low place, well-meaning people close to me attempted to help me see that Rachel's passing was not my fault. They were sincere in their attempts to help relieve me of my guilt, but I would not have it. In my mind I thought, *How do you know that I did my best? You were not there. You did not see how I could have chosen differently.* The truth of the matter is that I made a lot of mistakes and that I was, and am, selfish in the core of my being. The truth is that I could never be good enough. No matter how hard I tried, that simply was not, and is not, possible.

The truth is that most of us want to believe that we are better than we are; however, this is a fallacy. The Bible tells us that "there is not one righteous, no not one." Through Adam, sin entered the world, and we have inherited a sin nature from Adam. Have you ever wondered why young children do not have to be taught to lie or engage in devious behaviors, and why bad behaviors come naturally to them? We sin because we were born into sin as the Bible clearly states. And because we still have our sin nature (until we are called home with Christ), we make lots of mistakes despite our best attempts not to. Remember the apostle Paul when he acknowledged grappling with his sinful nature? "I do not understand what I do. For what I want to do I do not do, but what I hate I do" (Romans 7:15). But, praise God, the Bible provides us with hope and freedom when we acknowledge that we are sinners saved by grace through God's Son, Jesus. Jesus is our Redeemer who has redeemed us from our sinful state, and He redeems all the stupid and selfish things we do or could ever do. Fully accepting this concept about myself—that as hard as I tried to get everything right as Rachel's mom, that as long as I was living in a fallen world with a sinful nature, I would never be perfect—was the turning point for me, and it was the beginning of allowing God to lift me out of the dark pit of guilt and shame.

## He Lifted Me out of the Slimy Pit

When I was asked by a psychologist about how I felt when standing in the courtroom and facing the person responsible for ending Rachel's life, I was shocked at my response. I realized that I had no room for anger toward this young man who had made the decision that early morning to commit a terrible act against my daughter because I was too angry at myself. I clearly remember standing in the courtroom reading my victim's statement, and all I could feel was my own guilt. As I looked more closely and explored what was going on in my heart, I realized later that I had been in this dark place for quite some time after Rachel passed away because I blamed myself entirely. I could finally *allow* the Lord to lift me up out of the guilt that I was living with.

How often do we not allow for God's goodness in our lives because we consciously, or subconsciously, deem ourselves unworthy because of our past mistakes? How many of us push God out of our lives and replace Him with poor substitutes because we are burdened with guilt and shame? What would happen if we came to Him and confessed all our mistakes and failures? What would it look like for us to be unburdened of all of the wrongs that we have committed against ourselves and others? What would it look like to fall down at the foot of the cross and lay it all down there? The cross is the mercy of God toward us. This is the place where we can find our true worth. This is the place where we no longer need to carry the burden of guilt. And this is the place where we are worthy of all of God's goodness.

You may not be wrestling with the heavy weight of guilt and shame, or maybe it's there but you keep pushing it down because it is too painful to look at. You may be carrying around the guilt of mistakes you've made or wearing shame for the times when you have drifted away from the Lord and "acted out" like the prodigal son who squandered all the good things that his father had given him. Maybe you are telling yourself, "I have no burdens" or "I have no regrets." Is it possible that if we sit still long enough and listen to God's quiet voice within, without drugs, alcohol, shopping, working, relationships, etc., we will begin to see all of the "yuck" that we have buried deep within ourselves?

As long as we carry our mistakes around with us, we will be unable to experience the true freedom that God has for us. I was finally able to accept that I am a sinner saved by grace, and I make mistakes as a parent because I am, by nature, a sinner. Embracing this truth allowed me to reach up and allow my Savior to lift me up out of the pit of guilt and shame. He took hold of my hand, lifted me up out of that dark place, and "set my feet on a rock and gave me a firm place to stand."

## He Put a New Song in My Mouth

Coming up out of that pit was another step toward true heal-ing. And much more healing would follow as I learned to praise Him in my pain. "Lift your eyes up. Where does your help come from?" became the lyrics to my theme song. Lifting my eyes and heart up to the Lord is truly where my help has come from—over and over again. And without a doubt, I know that I would not be where I am today without His mighty hand of help and de-liverance in my life. The struggle is real—no question about it! The pain is there, and grieving is a process. But God put a *new song* in my heart after he lifted me out of the slimy pit of guilt and shame. The new song that he put in my heart felt different from any other song of praise that I have experienced in my lifetime. This song of praise would provide me with strength to journey on.

When God delivers us from the dark places, whether we were there because of the loss of a loved one or because of some other tragedy, God places a song of praise in our hearts. And as we praise Him, we receive the strength to continue on the road to healing. Because there are so many ups and downs we go through after losing a child or another loved one, we need strength for the duration of the grieving process. As I have shared with many clients and patients over the years, grieving is a process and not a "sprint" to the finish line. Grieving the loss of our loved ones is more like a marathon because we are in the process for the long haul.

We will face different stages of grief, and we will circle back around to stages of grief that we thought we were finished with—just to realize that we are there again. One stage, or aspect, of the grieving process is anger. Feeling angry is a natural human emotion, and it is often justified. But when anger takes up permanent residence in our hearts, we can become stuck, not proceeding forward in our healing.

# Chapter 6

## I'm So Angry

As surely as God lives, who has denied me justice, the Almighty, who has made me taste bitterness of soul, as long as I have life within me, the breath of God in my nostrils, my lips will not speak wickedness, and my tongue will utter no deceit. ... I will maintain my righteousness and never let go of it; my conscience will not reproach me as long as I live.

—Job 27:2–4, 6

As I have already shared, anger is a natural human emotion in response to injustice, tragic losses, and the terrible occurrences that happen in our world. We can see an angry response from Job in the passage at the start of this chapter. Here we see Job wrestling with the unjust losses he suffered and "the bitterness of soul" that God allowed him to experience—even though he was a "blameless man." As we can clearly see from the book of Job, he lost everything. All of Job's children died (in one tragic event), all of his wealth was lost, and his physical health was attacked by Satan. We also see that even though Job did not understand why the terrible tragedies had come upon him, he stayed committed to maintaining his righteousness (right standing with God). But for Job not to have experienced any anger in response to all the losses and injustices would have been unnatural. Job was human, just like you and me, and he experienced deep sorrow, grief, and anger.

Anger is part of the grieving process. We can experience anger toward ourselves, others, and God. Anger is not a bad thing in and of itself, and indeed anger is often righteous and justified. With all that said, what is most important is what we do with our anger. For instance, have you ever spoken with someone who was filled with so much anger that you were left with heaviness in your heart after you left them? This type of anger can become toxic and unhealthy for the individual who carries around that anger for too long.

Many years ago at the young age of fifteen, I visited a boyfriend every day in the hospital. My boyfriend had been in a terrible motorcycle accident that resulted in brain trauma injury. For three months I visited him while he lay unresponsive in a coma state. At the time I smoked cigarettes, and I took smoke breaks on the patio off the seventh-floor hospital unit. On one particular afternoon I was out on the patio, and a woman in a wheelchair was also on a smoke break, assisted by a nurse. This patient was blind, was unable to walk, and was dying. Unfortunately, she had an inoperable brain tumor that had stolen her sight, had put her in a wheelchair, and would eventually rob her of her life. What struck me about this woman was her intense anger. Within a short time of being in her presence, I'd heard her story. I heard her curse God and curse life. I literally shook from the inside as I experienced this woman's anger. I walked away that day with a fear of ever being that angry, to the point of the anger consuming me. Today I am thankful for that experience and the lasting impression of witnessing the impact that such a toxic and unhealthy anger can have on a person.

## Bitterness of Soul

After losing Rachel, I experienced anger intensely and in unexpected ways. From the very beginning, after surrendering my heart and life to Christ, I have not blamed God or been angry with Him. I did not blame God for the loss of my marriage or for the many other hurts and betrayals I experienced. But for a brief moment, about two weeks after Rachel passed away, I experienced what is known as "bitterness of soul." And unexpectedly, I had this surge of anger toward God rise up in my heart.

I was riding as a passenger in my car when my boyfriend and I were heading back from out of town. Out of nowhere, I suddenly felt furious with God. *Why did You allow this to happen? Haven't I served You with a committed heart for many years?* Anger overwhelmed me as the full force of the pain of losing Rachel hit me again. Other questions came pouring out with desperation to understand why. Why this? Sobs and weeping followed. Then came surrender to the God in whom I have put my trust. I had no answers and no resolution. But I knew then, and I know now, that He can be trusted with our greatest heartbreaks.

By the time my boyfriend and I arrived at our destination, the anger had subsided and was replaced with the words that I have lived by from the time I first committed my life to the Lord: "No matter what, I'm going to serve You." This was a "no matter what" situation. Did I really mean that I would live for Him all of my days, or was it conditional, based on what He would do or not do for me?

Many folks struggle with anger toward God. I have had a lot of clients and patients over the years who, like that angry woman in the hospital, become consumed with their anger, especially at God. I am also reminded of a couple who lost their son tragically about five years before I lost Rachel. My path crossed with this couple just weeks after losing Rachel, and when they heard that I had lost my daughter, they shared with me about how they had lost their son. They were so bitter and angry—so angry at the person who was responsible for their son's death. As the months and years passed and I continued working through my pain and anger, I would stop from time to time to visit them. Sadly, they were just as angry and bitter as the day I met them. My heart hurt for them. One afternoon I was provided the opportunity to share with the wife my hope in Christ. I shared with her that the Lord is my strength and my hope for healing. I pray those words have taken root in her heart.

## "I Will Maintain My Righteousness and Never Let Go of It"

My anger was directed at myself and at others in those early months, even the first two or three years (and if I am honest, I can go there again easily). I felt angry at pretty much everyone. I am not proud of this, but I am just being honest.

I was angry at the friends who were absent when Rachel struggled through the loss of her fiancé. I was angry at the church for not being more attentive (especially when they knew what she was going through). And I was angry at my friends who, after a few months, did not talk about Rachel and appeared indifferent to what I was going through. I sat paralyzed at the end of my world as I knew it, and I felt very angry about being in a horrible space that I did not want to be in.

Aware of my anger, especially as a therapist, I knew the dangers of getting "stuck" in my anger, so I forced myself and worked hard at connecting with people. But unfortunately this did not always go over well, especially in the early days.

On one specific occasion, I met up with a few girlfriends for a dinner out, something that a small group of us would do about once a month. About two months had passed since Rachel died, and I only agreed to go because I thought getting out would be helpful. During our conversation one of the friends began bemoaning the fact that her two grown sons were going away for about nine months to the mission field. She went on and talked about how she didn't know how she would manage their absence for that length of time. As I stared at her from across the table, I thought, *How dare you talk about your grief over missing your kids when they will only be gone for a matter of months. You will see them again. I buried my daughter only a couple of months ago, and I will not see her again in this lifetime.* The problem is that I didn't just think it; I actually said it aloud, and the table went silent.

One friend with tears streaming down her face apologized, but the insensitive friend who was so sad about her sons going away for a mission trip never apologized. And I don't think she had any insight into what I was experiencing as a grieving mom who had just buried her child. In fact, I have been astounded at the very unhelpful and insensitive words that people have said to me over the years after losing Rachel.

So many people have little to no insight into what a person is going through when they have lost a child or another loved one. I have also experienced people close to me demonstrate impatience with my grief and my pain, feeling that I should be "over it already." And still others just won't bring up Rachel's name.

Most people do not consider how I am doing around the

holidays, her birthday, or the anniversary date of her passing. People just do not understand. And how could they possibly understand? We cannot expect people to understand something so horrible unless they themselves have been through the loss of a child or another loved one. We can try to imagine what it's like, but imagining is incomparable to actually losing your child or another loved one.

As hurt and angry as I have been, I had to recognize that moving past the anger was vital to my physical, mental, and spiritual health. I did not want to stay angry. I wanted to "maintain my righteousness and never let go of it." I wanted to stay in close relationship with my heavenly Father, and I wanted to continue to live my life for Him "as long as I had breath."

The truth is that we will never get over losing our child or another loved one, but we can heal and move beyond the anger. I share with my patients that it is not the passage of time that heals the wounds, but rather how we spend that time. We have to work at it. The anger does not always resolve on its own. In fact, when a tragedy like the loss of a child or another loved one strikes, anger usually wants to stick around and take up permanent residence in our hearts.

Today, over nine years after losing Rachel, I still work at keeping my anger in check. I don't always succeed at this, but I am much farther along than I was nine years ago. How about you? Where are you at today with your anger? Are you in the same place you were when the tragedy happened, or have you moved closer to letting go of the anger? As I shared in the beginning of this chapter, anger is a natural emotion in response to a terrible and unjust occurrence, but when the anger lingers, it becomes toxic to our physical, mental, and spiritual well-being.

# A Matter of Perspective

In this section I'd like to have a candid discussion with you, my reader, about *how* we move past our anger. The passage at the beginning of this chapter is a tough one for a lot of people, but I chose the passage for the distinct purpose of addressing this very important topic. We can clearly see in this passage, and in other passages in the book of Job, that God allowed for the tragic losses that Job suffered. There is no getting around this.

Much has been written about "Where is God when bad things happen?" and "Why do bad things happen to good people?" I will not attempt to answer these theological questions because many qualified people have already written excellent books on this subject. Furthermore, my aim is to bring you hope by demonstrating how God graciously and faithfully led me through the most devastating and painful time in my life. As I approach this discussion, I do so with great respect for your loss and for your pain. And I do not take lightly what you have walked through because I too have experienced the "bitterness of soul" and have drunk "from the cup of suffering." I can honestly say that I understand your struggle with the question of where God is in all this.

Some of us remain stuck in our anger longer than others, and some of us experience greater anger at ourselves, at others, or at God. As you have read my story about losing my daughter, you can see that I got stuck in my anger for a season, and my anger was primarily directed at myself and secondly at others. Some folks do not experience anger at themselves, at others, or at God; everyone is different and experiences their losses differently. You are not "bad," "less than," or "less spiritual" because of how you are experiencing your anger. One person may not experience a lot of anger after their loss—and there is nothing wrong with that, so we should not take issue with them and try to make them feel something that they do not need to feel.

Wherever you are with your anger, I believe that it is a matter of perspective that will allow you to move past the anger and come to a place of acceptance. I also believe that Job's suffering was a lesson and directive for all of us. Job's perspective of his losses, pain, and suffering allowed him to continue in his relationship with God, which is the opposite of what Satan had anticipated. Satan's plan was to destroy Job's heart toward God, and I imagine that he wanted Job to turn away from God and curse Him for all his loss and suffering. Even though God allowed for the tragic losses in Job's life, Satan is the one who inflicted the suffering with the intent to destroy Job's relationship with God. How often have we seen this in people's lives who have experienced loss and suffering? I certainly have in my work as a therapist over the years.

In the first chapter of the book of Job, Satan points out to God that the only reason that Job is blameless and upright before God is because God has blessed Job, but if Job were to lose his blessings, he would curse God. In response to this, God says to Satan, "Very well, then, everything he has is in your hands, but on the man himself, do not lay a finger" (Job 1:12).

As we continue to read in chapter 1, Job experiences the loss of all his wealth and all his children, but he still does not curse God as Satan had predicted. Instead, "Job tore his robe and shaved his head. Then he fell to the ground in worship and said, naked I came from my mother's womb, and naked I will depart. The Lord gave and the Lord has taken away; may the name of the Lord be praised. In all of this, Job did not sin by *charging God with wrongdoing*" (Job 1:20–22, emphasis added).

Satan went back to God and said that if Job were to be struck in his "flesh and bones, he will surely curse you to your face" (Job 2:5). So again, God allows Satan to afflict Job: "So Satan went out from the presence of the Lord and afflicted Job with painful sores from the soles of his feet to the top of his head" (Job 2:7). Job still would not curse God, though his wife said to him, "Are you still holding on to your integrity? Curse God and die" (Job 2:9)! I love Job's response: "You are talking like a foolish woman. *Shall we accept good from God, and not trouble*" (emphasis added)?

Job's perspective was that he would continue to serve God in times of blessing and in times of loss and suffering. He acknowledged that God had allowed for the tragedies in his life. He may not have been able to explain exactly why God had allowed such things, but he trusted the God he served.

How is your perspective influencing your anger? Do you see God as the bad guy who allowed your child or other loved one to die? Or do you trust the God you have served and believed in, even though He has allowed loss and suffering in your life? Do you trust that He sees the entire picture of your life and your loved one's life? Job *willfully* chose how he would perceive his tragic circumstances. My dear friend, how will *you* choose to perceive your tragic circumstances and the loss of your loved one?

# Chapter 7

Must I Forgive?

Then Peter came to Jesus and asked, Lord, how
many times shall I forgive my brother when he sins
against me? Up to seven times? Jesus answered, I
tell you, not seven times, but seventy times seven.

—Matthew 18:21–22

*M*oving beyond our anger includes a very critical compo-
nent: forgiveness. Forgiveness is not about the words that
we speak. Instead, forgiveness goes much deeper than that.
Forgiveness is a matter of the heart. Jesus said in Matthew 18:35,
"Forgive your brother from the heart."

I clearly recall when I surrendered my heart and life to the
Lord at age nineteen. With the heavy burden of anger and bitterness in my heart, I began attending a small church where I
was discipled by people who cared about me. They were older
and grounded in their faith. The congregation believed in the
power of prayer, and I often sought prayer for areas in which I
struggled. One such area was that of forgiveness. I harbored anger and hate in my heart, and I did not realize how destructive
carrying around these emotions was to me. And I did not know

how to forgive someone for causing hurt to my heart or under-stand why I even had to.

## The Process of Forgiveness

Throughout my life I have had the opportunity to forgive people or hold resentments against them. Some offenses that I have been faced with were small offenses, whereas others were quite major. I would prefer to say that I have been consistent and diligent about following what Jesus instructed us to do in Matthew concerning the forgiveness of people, but I haven't been. I will often think that I have forgiven someone, and then resentments come back up in my heart, and I realize that I am still in the process of forgiving them. Forgiveness is more often than not a process, especially when the offense and hurt has been great. This means that the forgiveness of another person can take some time, and we may have to reassess as we go through the process of forgiveness in order to track our progress in this area.

Over the past nine years since losing my daughter Rachel, I have had to look honestly, at times with great difficulty, at where my heart is in the forgiveness process. Moving through the anger toward people and toward myself was the beginning of true forgiveness—not only forgiveness of the people whom I had blamed and been angry with, but also forgiveness of myself. Not having myself "on trial" any longer has freed me to continue my journey of grieving and healing.

When we hold on to hate and anger, we are stunted in our capacity to forgive. Consequently, we remain stuck in our pain and suffering. Remember the woman I encountered in the hospital who was so full of anger and hate? She was truly stuck in her own suffering. In many ways we could say, "Well, who can blame her? What a horrible situation for her to have to endure—and just to die at the end." And the couple who lost their son, did they have a right to be angry with the person responsible for their son's death? Of course they did. But holding on to their anger precluded forgiveness. And they remained in the same place with their pain and suffering as they were on the day they received the news that he had been killed. Very sad!

## Making the Choice to Forgive

As we read through scripture, we see that the Bible has a lot to say about forgiveness—in both the Old Testament and in the New Testament. The passage of scripture that opens this chapter, where Peter is asking Jesus how many times we are to forgive someone, Peter proposes seven times to forgive someone. He was being more generous than the rabbis, who only required three times to forgive. But Jesus is saying that we must continue to forgive—there is no limit to how many times we are required to forgive. Forgiveness is a choice, a choice to follow the directives of the Lord. Forgiveness is also quite possibly one of the most difficult choices we make in our lives and in our walk with God, especially when we have lost a loved one.

## Forgiveness Is about God's Mercy

Forgiveness is about so much more than forgiving someone who has hurt or wronged us. Forgiveness is about God's mercy toward us. We witness Jesus's mercy toward "undeserving" sinners throughout His ministry on earth.

One of my favorite incidents where Jesus demonstrates His mercy through the forgiveness of sin is found in John 8:3–8: "The teachers of the law and the Pharisees brought in a woman caught in the act of adultery. They made her stand before the group and said to Jesus, 'Teacher, this woman was caught in the act of adultery. In the Law Moses commanded us to stone such women. Now what do you say?'" They were using this question as a trap in order to have a basis for accusing Him. But Jesus bent down and started to write on the ground with His finger. When they kept on questioning Him, He straightened up and said, "If any one of you is without sin, let him be the first to throw a stone at her." Again He stooped down and wrote on the ground. Jesus was making the point very clearly that this woman's sins were no different from the sins of those accusing her. I suspect that maybe Jesus was listing their sins in the dirt, making the point that they too had sinned. And the only individual present who was in the position to condemn this woman was Jesus. However, we see Him extend forgiveness and mercy toward her. I love Jesus's beautiful words to her: "Woman, where are they? Has no one condemned you?"

"No, sir," she replied.

"Then neither do I condemn you. Go now, and leave your life of sin."

These teachers of the law and the Pharisees did something that we continue to do today: we judge others' sin as worse than our own sin. What a powerful illustration of how "we have all sinned and fallen short of the glory of God." Another very striking example of forgiveness and mercy that Jesus demonstrated is found in Luke 23:34. As Jesus was dying on the cross, He uttered the words, "Father forgive them, for they know not what they do." What incredible mercy Jesus showed to those who had nailed Him to the cross. Those who stood there mocking him—it was their sin that He was hanging on that cross for. He was an innocent man! And yet He asked His Father to forgive them for their horrible treatment of Him. I believe that He had all of us in mind when He spoke those words of mercy. In His darkest hours, taking the sins of the world upon Himself, He showed us His love, mercy, and forgiveness.

Again, the Lord demonstrated His mercy through forgiveness when He responded to the thief hanging on the cross next to Him. The criminal, close to death, called out, "Jesus, remember me when You come into Your kingdom." And Jesus answered him, "I tell you the truth, today you will be with Me in paradise." Astonishing! This man acknowledged his sin and accepted his punishment, and he entered heaven that day a free man. And just like the thief on the cross next to Jesus, the adulterous woman walked free of her shame and guilt. Forgiveness brings freedom.

## Forgiveness Frees

Forgiveness frees us, the forgiver, and it can also free the offender. Over the years I have worked with numerous folks from various backgrounds whom I found to be imprisoned in their own world of resentment and unforgiveness. Even when people are not religious or faith affiliated, unforgiveness affects them the same way. But I have also worked with people who experience true freedom from the heavy burden of hurt and pain. This happens when folks are able to go through the process of forgiveness.

In my own life, I have embraced the amazing joy of walking free from childhood pain because I chose the path of forgiveness. But this path has most definitely involved challenging and difficult periods. And today, as I continue to work through my anger surrounding my daughter's death, I am much farther along in the process of forgiveness. However, I would not consider myself there yet, but by God's grace I will continue the process (especially toward the young man responsible for my daughter's death). I realize that I cannot do this without God's help and His empowerment. So I will pray for myself in the process, and I pray for those whom I need to forgive. I want God's heart for them— yes, even for the young man who committed a terrible act that early morning, resulting in Rachel's death.

## Far-Reaching Effects of Forgiveness

Letting go of bitterness and resentments and choosing forgiveness instead can have far-reaching effects that go beyond just the forgiver and offender. Let's take a look at an amazing example of how forgiveness can reach far and wide, beyond ourselves. Many of us are familiar with the story of Joseph in the book of Genesis. Joseph was envied and hated by his brothers because he had his father's favor. So Joseph's brothers devised a plan to get rid of him. They initially planned to kill him, but they decided to sell him into slavery instead (Genesis 37). As a result of his brother's actions, Joseph ended up as a servant in the house of Potiphar.

Joseph found favor with Potiphar, and Potiphar saw that "the Lord was with him, and gave him success in everything he did." Potiphar promoted Joseph, putting him in charge of his entire household and all that Potiphar owned. In time, Potiphar's wife made several advances toward Joseph, asking him to sleep with her. Joseph refused each time, and with the final advance from Potiphar's wife, he fled from her, leaving his cloak behind. After Joseph fled, Potiphar's wife called the household servants and accused Joseph of trying to take advantage of her. When Potiphar arrived home, she showed him the cloak and told him, "That Hebrew slave you brought us came to me to make sport of me. But as soon as I screamed for help, he left his cloak beside me and ran out of the house" (Genesis 39:17–18). Potiphar "burned with anger" and put Joseph in prison (Genesis 39:20).

Both of these incidents, being sold into slavery by his brothers and being falsely accused by Potiphar's wife, could have resulted in Joseph's resentment, bitterness, and unforgiveness toward his brothers and Potiphar's wife. Especially since Joseph was an innocent man who honored God with his life. He was a man of honesty and integrity. I imagine that Joseph had moments of discouragement and anger (after all, he was human) because of the injustices that had been committed against him. I also imagine that during those years that Joseph spent in slavery and in prison, he had ample opportunity to develop bitterness and resentment toward those who had caused him such pain and suffering.

If Joseph had not chosen the path of forgiveness, he would not have experienced the freedom and success that God had blessed him with. Furthermore, on a far-reaching scale, all of Egypt and Joseph's family were saved from a seven-year famine. Because of Joseph's willingness to forgive in spite of the injustice, pain, and suffering he had experienced, all of Egypt was spared, including Joseph and his entire family.

What if Joseph had chosen to stay angry, and what if he had chosen to hold on to resentment, bitterness, and unforgiveness toward his brothers and Potiphar's wife? Would all have perished during the famine? Yes, quite possibly! But God continued to use Joseph and blessed him with great success. At the age of thirty, Joseph was put in charge of all of Egypt, right under the pharaoh.

God has used many amazing, and ordinary, people over the years to do great deeds in His name, and He has used these people to make life-changing differences in our world. We know that the people whom God uses to do extraordinary acts, just like

Joseph, have had to choose the path of forgiveness. In Joseph's situation, we see that he was beautifully reunited with his brothers, and he graciously extended God's mercy and forgiveness toward all of them. In response to the forgiveness and grace that Joseph extended to his brothers, the brothers demonstrated true repentance for what they had done to Joseph. When forgiveness happens, reconciliation is also made possible, such as in this case of Joseph and his brothers.

On the other hand, reconciliation is not always possible. And reconciliation with the offender, or the person responsible for your pain and suffering, may not be necessarily best for you. You may have well-meaning people in your life instructing you to reconcile a relationship with an individual whom you have forgiven. May I just say that forgiveness does not always mean allowing folks access to your life, especially if they have caused you great pain. They may be unrepentant and unchanged.

## What Forgiveness Is Not

As we have discussed at length what forgiveness means and why forgiveness is so important, let us now look at what forgiveness is not. Forgiveness does not mean that we are fine with the wrongful acts of or committed by another person. Nor does forgiveness mean that there should be no consequences for the wrongful actions. Furthermore, forgiveness does not mean that we must reconcile with people who have hurt us. For instance, if you have someone in your life, a friend or family member, who has hurt you in some way, you will need to work through the process of forgiveness. And no matter what the person's response to you is, your commitment to the process of forgiveness needs to remain. Sometimes the people we are forgiving are toxic and unsafe people. And sometimes people can bring their chaos into our lives. These are individuals we need to keep at a healthy distance, even if they are family members.

Over the years I have worked with patients and clients who have felt obligated to allow family members access to their lives just because they are family. When working on the process of forgiveness, we need to assess whether or not the family member or friend is someone who should have access to our lives. Oftentimes, just setting and maintaining very good boundaries with friends and family members, limiting our time with them, can be the solution to experiencing further pain from them. But unfortunately many of us have family members who are extremely toxic and who continue to cause pain and suffering, whether they intend to or not. These folks should not have access to our lives, especially if they are resistant to change.

As I have worked with patients experiencing the effects of destructive and abusive childhoods, all too often I am witness to the deep psychological wounds in the hearts and souls of these people, which linger for years into adulthood. These patients demonstrate immense courage as they work through their trauma and begin the process of forgiveness. And for many of these folks, the damage is too great for them to continue in a relationship with their offenders. Forgiveness does not mean that the family member, or any other person, gets a free pass for what they have done to you. If you have been hurt by someone or if you have experienced the loss of a loved one at the hands of another person, the decision is entirely yours if you will allow them into your life. You are the one who knows how this individual has affected, and continues to affect, you. And you are not wrong or unforgiving for wanting to see justice served or for not wanting your offender to be a part of your life. And you are not lacking empathy or lacking in God's love for moving on in a direction away from the person who has wounded you or your loved one.

After the loss of my daughter Rachel, my family and I had to participate in criminal court proceedings, working with the district attorney's (DA) office. We were provided the opportunity to share with the DA's office what outcome we wished for the young man who was responsible for Rachel's death. Crime scene investigators found clear evidence of intentionality at the accident site, writing in their report that the driver of the car had intentionally driven his vehicle into a large traffic light pole at approximately seventy to eighty miles per hour. My daughter was in the passenger seat and was pronounced dead at the scene. Even with the evidence and the police reports listing the incident as murder and homicide, the DA's office informed us the charge would be manslaughter.

How shocking and astonishing that victims have such little say in what punishment or consequences their offender receives. As my family and I sat around the large oval-shaped table, located close to the courtroom where we would read our victims' statements, we were stunned. *Manslaughter. ... That's it? ... That's all?! But he murdered my daughter! I do not understand.* We were asked to agree to these terms to avoid a trial, and the attorney firmly stated that he would not get anything more than manslaughter even with a trial—and then we would have to go through the horribleness of a trial. When the manslaughter charge was presented before the judge in the courtroom, he had a problem with such a minimal charge. The judge called counsel into his chambers, but the manslaughter charge stuck. And unfortunately justice was not served! The young man ended up serving only three months in jail.

What a devastating blow to all of us. We walked out of the

courtroom that day weeping over the injustice that had just taken place. This injustice was wrong, and the pain of losing Rachel hurt even more with the knowledge that the person responsible for her death would soon walk free. When family members do not receive justice for their loved one's death, the process of healing and forgiveness can be more difficult. My family, unfortunately, are not the only ones who have experienced such injustice. Too many families also live with this pain. But I want to bring the discussion back around to us, you and me—the victims of injustice and wrongdoing.

My concern is for us. I want to see our hearts healing. I want us walking free from anger, bitterness, and resentment, and I want us to begin the process of forgiveness. I want forgiveness to take the place of destructive emotions in each of our hearts so that we can move forward in our own freedom. Once we are freed from the unforgiveness that once ruled our minds and hearts, we can be used by God to make an incredible difference in the world and in the lives of many fellow sojourners.

Absolutely, without a doubt, if I had not worked through the anger and begun the process of forgiveness, I would not be in a place to help other wounded and hurting people. And I definitely would not have written *Saving Grace.* So your question for me may be, how did you do it? How have you forgiven people from your past, and how are you able to forgive the person responsible for your daughter's death?

## The Secret to Forgiveness

Please allow me to return to what I shared at the beginning of this chapter about my own process of forgiveness when I was just a new Christian and struggling with the concept of forgiveness.

As I wrestled in my mind with how it is possible to forgive someone for such horrible offenses, this is what Jesus laid on my heart to do: *pray for them!* He graciously showed me this was the beginning of forgiveness. Amazingly I would not have thought of doing this because why would I want to pray for someone whom I detested and hated? Sheesh, that's not exactly the thought I had in mind. I had my own dark thoughts about people who had caused me pain over the years. But God in His amazing wisdom knew the condition of my heart (very hardened), and He knew what it would take to prepare and soften my heart. At first, I begrudgingly whispered a forced prayer through my teeth, wondering why I had to do this. After all, those who had harmed me did not deserve my prayers, much less my forgiveness (obviously I had not read *Saving Grace*). I continued to pray for the people I had issues with simply out of obedience to what God had put in my heart to do. I had absolutely no desire to pray these prayers. But in a relatively short amount of time, an interesting development occurred. Now the prayers that I prayed were prayed with more willingness, and they were no longer prayed through clenched teeth. And I was experiencing less resistance each time I entered into this place of prayer for others. What followed was miraculous. Each time I entered into prayer for my offenders, I wept for them, my heart was literally breaking for them. What was happening to me? My heart had become God's heart for every person for whom I had obediently been praying. No more hatred or bitterness could be found within me; true forgiveness was now a condition of my heart. I had forgiven! And the wonders that followed in my life as a result of forgiveness and freedom—well, that's for another book.

## How about You, Dear Friend?

I understand your struggle firsthand, and I do not take lightly your pain and suffering or the terrible loss you have experienced. Writing this chapter was a tough decision to make, and I prayed carefully with you in mind before writing it. In fact, I had originally planned for another chapter in place of this one, but God directed me otherwise. I understand how insensitive people can be when they talk about our need to forgive others. One individual scolded me for being angry and heartbroken at the lack of justice in my daughter's case. I understand the agony of facing our offender, praying for them, and letting go of our anger, bitterness, and hatred toward them. I understand, my friend; I truly do. But I have written *Saving Grace* for you, and I have candidly and vulnerably shared my pain, suffering, and loss with you—all for the purpose of encouraging you to grieve, heal, and move forward in freedom. God has much in store for you, and he has much for you to do in your life. Imagine what you and I can accomplish! As with Joseph, if we let go of our anger and embrace the process of forgiveness, then the possibilities are limitless.

# Chapter 8

## *Meaning and Purpose Again: Moving Forward*

Do you not know? Have you not heard? The Lord is the everlasting God, the Creator of the ends of the earth. He will not grow tired or weary, and His understanding no one can fathom. He gives strength to the weary and increases the power of the weak. Even youths grow tired and weary, and young men stumble and fall; but those who hope in The Lord will renew their strength. They will soar on wings like eagles; they will run and not grow weary, they will walk and not be faint.

—Isaiah 40:28–31

*I*n those early months, and even for several years, after Rachel passed away, I struggled to find meaning and purpose in life. The moment I received the news that my daughter had been killed, I felt as though my own life slipped away from me. I went around feeling like a shell, disconnected from everything and everyone.

In one of my journal entries, about five weeks after Rachel was gone, I wrote, "I am sinking and will never come up to normal again. ... I feel like I have completely disconnected from people and God." Another entry, this one written in the fifth month after her passing, reads, "I fear I will never be the same, like my heart will never want to live again." And on the third anniversary of Rachel's passing, my journal entry included the words, "Nothing in this world appeals to me."

During these early months and years, I experienced crazy ups and downs in my mood. Sometimes I felt that I had a handle on my grieving, and the next moment I was in a very dark place again. How I felt from day to day, and at times moment to moment, was often uncertain. The lack of predictability with my mood made planning daily activities very challenging. I went from feeling alive and active to feeling as though all the color in life had disappeared and been replaced with shades of gray. One moment I was "doing life," and the next moment I felt that I'd been run over by a steamroller, dumping me in the middle of an emotional wilderness.

## He Gives Strength to the Weary

The road to "coming back to life" has been the most painful and difficult of any road that I have ever had to travel down. I experienced weariness in my mind, body, and spirit, but I kept getting up each day and doing what I thought I was supposed to be doing, often feeling robotic. I sought counseling at different stages of my grief, especially when I could not move forward in a particular area of my grieving process. As a therapist, I realized that counseling or therapy would be an important part of my journey, especially at different stages of my grieving.

Most important is that I clung to the promise in Isaiah, and I knew that God would give me strength for my weary soul. This particular passage in Isaiah has held much meaning and influence in my life over the years, from the beginning of my walk with Christ.

When I first gave my life to Christ at age nineteen, I was very weary from life. In those early days, I would take my Bible and a cassette tape player and go to the top of this hill that overlooked the city. I would listen to a beautiful rendition of this passage in Isaiah being sung by a gifted male vocalist. There, on that hilltop, with tears streaming down my nineteen-year-old face, the foundation of my faith in Christ was built! There, alone with my God, I developed a strong awareness of His presence, a place I could find refuge in. And it was there on that hilltop that God showed me that He would always be there for me, renewing my strength for my journey as I placed my hope in Him. Little did I know that this mountaintop experience would prepare me for what would be the most tragic of all situations that I would ever face, the loss of my child.

## Hope in the Lord, the Renewal of Strength

Putting my hope in the Lord was a personal choice that I would have to make. No one else could make this choice for me. We are all free to choose what we will place our hope in. As I have already mentioned, people turn to various "pain relievers" to experience relief from the suffering that comes with the loss of a loved one. I have seen this countless times over the years working with patients. I see people use drugs, alcohol, sex, relationships, careers, shopping, and busyness. But unfortunately these are all temporary masks for the pain that we are in. And many of these substitutes lead to greater, more complex problems that we will have to face eventually and come to terms with.

In my pain I used substitutes and behaviors in my attempts to minimize my suffering, and not all of my choices were healthy or helpful. I would very much like to tell you that I got it right every time. I would like to tell you that I had the "faith that could move mountains," but making that claim would be dishonest and misleading. I would also like to say that in my day-to-day functioning I used better coping skills such as exercise, prayer, Bible reading, worship, connecting with trustworthy and sensitive people, and listening to positive, uplifting messages that led to healthier thought processes. But I need to be transparent and honest with you because we are real people with real pain.

I want you as my reader and my fellow sojourner to know that you are not alone in your desperate attempts to make it stop hurting. God is rich in mercy and grace, and He loves us no matter what poor choices we have made or are making. He loves us no matter what, and He wants only the very best for us. God knows better than anyone that our unhealthy choices do not bring healing to our broken hearts, and He knows the best way for us to move forward in our journey of grieving because He knows us better than we even know ourselves. Our heavenly Father truly knows best.

If you are a person who has made poor choices in your attempt to lessen the pain of losing your child or other loved one, you may be living with guilt and shame today. And you may have experienced judgment by well-meaning people around you for your "lack of faith." But please remember, my friend, people who have not experienced the devastating loss of a child or other loved one cannot possibly understand your pain. They may judge you for how you are handling your loss. But please turn your eyes to the compassionate and loving God who created you.

An important part of moving forward after the loss of a loved one is utilizing our capacity not to take the opinions of others personally or seriously. We definitely do not want to internalize the insensitive words of people who think they know what we need, or those who they think that they are the Holy Spirit, telling us what we ought to be doing.

We will always have people around us who lack empathy and who have little to no insight into our pain and suffering. After losing Rachel, I was amazed at some of the insensitive statements that people made. For instance, one woman (who was unable to bear children) said, "At least you have two other children." While this is true, and I am sure she did not mean to be hurtful, having two other children does not make up for or lessen the pain of losing my child. Yet another situation that you may encounter is when family and friends engage in avoidant behavior. I faced this more often than I would have ever guessed it would happen. From early on after Rachel passed away, some people (more than I care to admit) would not bring up the loss of Rachel. They would talk around the topic, speaking about everything and anything except my daughter's death. Again, most people are not intending to be hurtful or insensitive, but they are uncomfortable and do not know what to say, how to say it, or when to say it.

Learning how to manage people who are insensitive or critical of the way we are managing our loss is a very important part of our healing process. We often overlook this area for a variety of reasons. If we do not pay attention to our emotional reactions to others, we may get caught up in anger and find ways to justify holding on to our anger. But if we can step away from the hurtful words of well-meaning people, then we can step into God's amazing grace. We can seek His ways, His best, and His direction for our lives. We find our hope in Him, not in people.

In my experience, one of the most helpful and practical ways of placing my hope in God (which has proven to be a significant factor in moving me forward in my grieving process) has been my quiet alone time with God. "In your presence there is fullness of joy; at your right hand are pleasures forevermore" (Psalm 16:11 ESV). I have poured out my heart to Him, and I have wept bitterly before Him, knowing that He knows even when others do not and cannot know. And as I have lingered in His presence, doing what the psalmist said, "Be still and know that I am God" (Psalm 46:10), I have been refreshed and filled with renewed hope. As His Word promises us, if we put our hope in Him, He will renew our strength day by day.

## They Will Soar on Wings Like Eagles

Not only will He renew our strength as we place our hope in Him and wait on Him, but also He promises that we "will soar on wings like eagles" as we "hope in the Lord." What does it mean or look like to "soar like an eagle"?

Interestingly enough, God uses the analogy of the eagle in his description of who we can become. The eagle is considered to be a symbol of beauty, bravery, courage, honor, pride, determination, and grace. God specifically chose the eagle because of the eagle's specific characteristics. And these are characteristics that you and I can also possess as we "hope in the Lord," putting our trust in Him. God provides us not only with a picture of the beautiful qualities we can have that will allow us to soar above the storms in this life but also with the hope that we will move forward in our grieving process.

The eagle can soar to the greatest of heights and can travel long distances. The eagle uses what is called a wind thermal, which is a rising current of warm air, to achieve altitudes of up to ten thousand feet. How astounding! And what is particularly amazing, eagles, unlike other birds, have the ability to lock their wings in a fixed position and head into a fierce storm. The eagle catches wind thermals, taking the bird to higher altitudes with little effort. The higher altitudes are above the storm, where the eagle can glide in the calm. When I consider this analogy of the eagle, which God uses to describe how we can "soar on wings as eagles," I am amazed. And notice that He mentions the eagle's wings specifically. God is the one who designed their wings to allow them to soar in such conditions to higher altitudes, and He has created us with the same capacity to soar to higher altitudes in the midst of our storms, where we can glide above the storm.

We do not have literal wings like the eagle, of course, but our wings are the placing of our hope and trust in the Lord. As we wait, hope, and trust, we will soar to great altitudes, altitudes that we never imagined possible for us to reach. This is not wishful thinking (as some may be inclined to say). This is what God promises to us, His people.

Just as I began this chapter, sharing with you about our freedom to choose what direction we will go in with our pain and grief, I mention here that we are also free to choose where we will place our hope. If we choose to place our hope in the Lord, then we will soar to high places and will progress forward in our grieving and healing process. We will go on to do great things in His strength. Ever since I lost Rachel, my prayers have been, "Lord, please redeem this horrible tragedy, and please use me to help others who are hurting from the loss of their loved ones." I know that the enemy of my soul, Satan, the great deceiver, planned on my destruction through the loss of my daughter. In the Bible we read that "the thief comes to kill, steal and destroy, but I [Jesus] have come to give you life and give it to you more abundantly" (John 3:3). The Bible also says that "Satan goes around like a roaring lion seeking whom he may devour" (1 Peter 5:8).

If you are a person of faith and if you are about God's business, you are the one Satan would like to destroy. And guess what? He'd like to use the loss of your loved one to do it. But we have these wings called hope, wait, and trust that lift us to altitudes beyond our enemy's grasp.

For me, I chose to wait upon the Lord, putting my hope in Him. And now I am soaring to much higher altitudes than ever before. God has answered my prayers, and He is redeeming the loss of my daughter by allowing me to reach out to many people every day. This book that I am writing for you is part of that answer to my prayers. And I am typing *Saving Grace* on Rachel's laptop that I had bought for her just months before she passed away. I believe that Rachel would be pleased that I am using it to write this book in order to help a lot of hurting people (because she was all about helping hurting people).

## Hold on to Hope

God has come through just as He has done throughout my entire life, through every trial and through every storm. He has been there through the most difficult moments of my life. He has covered me with His saving grace in my darkest hours, those moments when I despaired of life. He has given me His strength and the hope to journey on. My dear friend, my sincere prayer for you, as I write this for *you*, is that you will "wait on the Lord," which literally means to *keep waiting*. This also means to put your hope in the Lord, trusting that He will redeem your loss the way that He has redeemed mine. As you continue to move forward, may the coming weeks, months, and years be a journey of hope and healing. God bless you always.

CPSIA information can be obtained
at www.ICGtesting.com
Printed in the USA
BVHW032254010621
608598BV00004B/26